SELECTION FOR
PIANO DUET

THE OLD GUMBIE CAT
BUSTOPHER JONES   OLD DEUTERONOMY
SKIMBLESHANKS   MEMORY
MR MISTOFFELEES

MUSIC BY

ANDREW LLOYD WEBBER

ARRANGED BY DANIEL SCOTT

FABER MUSIC LTD
3 QUEEN SQUARE, LONDON WC1N 3AU

Secondo
The Old Gumbie Cat

ANDREW LLOYD WEBBER
arr. DANIEL SCOTT

Legato (a Glenn Miller flavour) (♩ = c. 104)

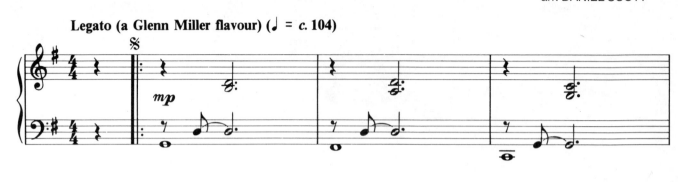

The Old Gumbie Cat

ANDREW LLOYD WEBBER
arr. DANIEL SCOTT

Legato (a Glenn Miller flavour) (♩ = c. 104)

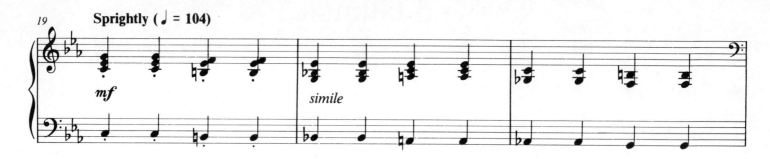

Bustopher Jones: the Cat about Town

ANDREW LLOYD WEBBER
arr. DANIEL SCOTT

Bustopher Jones: the Cat about Town

ANDREW LLOYD WEBBER
arr. DANIEL SCOTT

Tempo I

Secondo

Old Deuteronomy

ANDREW LLOYD WEBBER
arr. DANIEL SCOTT

Slow and sustained (♩. = 44)

con Ped.

Old Deuteronomy

ANDREW LLOYD WEBBER
arr. DANIEL SCOTT

Slow and sustained ($\downarrow$. = 44)

Skimbleshanks: the Railway Cat

ANDREW LLOYD WEBBER
arr. DANIEL SCOTT

Skimbleshanks: the Railway Cat

ANDREW LLOYD WEBBER
arr. DANIEL SCOTT

Secondo

Secondo

Memory

ANDREW LLOYD WEBBER
arr. DANIEL SCOTT

Memory

ANDREW LLOYD WEBBER
arr. DANIEL SCOTT

Secondo

Secondo

Mr Mistoffelees

ANDREW LLOYD WEBBER
arr. DANIEL SCOTT

Mr Mistoffelees

ANDREW LLOYD WEBBER
arr. DANIEL SCOTT